FAST Lane
OPEN-WHEEL RACING

SPRINT CARS

By Tyrone Georgiou

Gareth Stevens
Publishing

SPRINT CARS

Please visit our website, www.garethstevens.com. For a free color catalog of all our high-quality books, call toll free 1-800-542-2595 or fax 1-877-542-2596.

Library of Congress Cataloging-in-Publication Data

Georgiou, Tyrone.
Sprint cars / Tyrone Georgiou.
     p. cm. — (Fast lane: open-wheel racing)
Includes index.
ISBN 978-1-4339-5768-0 (pbk.)
ISBN 978-1-4339-5769-7 (6-pack)
ISBN 978-1-4339-5766-6 (library binding)
1. Sprint cars. I. Title.
TL236.27.G46 2012
796.72—dc22

                                        2011009418

First Edition

Published in 2012 by
Gareth Stevens Publishing
111 East 14th Street, Suite 349
New York, NY 10003

Copyright © 2012 Gareth Stevens Publishing

Designer: Daniel Hosek
Editor: Greg Roza

Photo credits: Cover, pp. 1, 4–5, 17 John Harrelson/Getty Images; p. 7 (main image) RacingOne/ISC Archives/Getty Images; p. 7 (Henry Ford) Getty Images; pp. 9, 12–13, 14–15 (main image), 19 Todd Warshaw/Getty Images; p. 11 Shutterstock.com; p. 15 (Eldora Speedway) Chris Graythen/Getty Images.

Printed in the United States of America

CPSIA compliance information: Batch #CS11GS: For further information contact Gareth Stevens, New York, New York at 1-800-542-2595.

CONTENTS

Words in the glossary appear in **bold** type the first time they are used in the text.

SATURDAY NIGHT!

It's Saturday night! Race fans across the United States, Canada, Australia, New Zealand, and South Africa head out to their local dirt tracks to see some exciting sprint car racing. Sliding sideways through the corners and shooting down the straights, these crazy cars with huge wings put on quite a show. Sprint cars send dirt flying with their powerful engines and mismatched tires. Slipping and sliding, bumping and crashing— there's nothing else like it!

Fast Fact   The World of Outlaws is one of the most popular sprint car series in the United States. It features some of the sport's biggest stars.

Sprint cars can reach speeds of about 140 miles (225 km) per hour!

5

SPRINT CAR HISTORY

The first sprint cars were built in the early 1900s just after World War I (1914–1918). Most were stripped-down Model T Fords, which were cheap and plentiful. During the 1930s, **mechanics** started building sprint cars from scratch. The cars grew larger and more powerful. **V-8 engines** became popular in the 1950s. The first winged cars showed up in 1958. However, there are still sprint car series that race without wings, just like in the old days of the sport.

Fast Fact

Henry Ford's Model T was the first mass-produced automobile. In the 19 years it was manufactured, more than 15 million Model Ts rolled off the **assembly line.**

Henry-Ford

Tommy Hinnerschitz leads a sprint car race in 1935.

7

INSIDE SPRINT CARS

Sprint cars have a short **wheelbase** that's only 84 to 90 inches (213 to 229 cm). This helps them turn and slide. The right rear tire is larger than the left rear tire. That's because the right side has a little further to go since it's on the outside as the car speeds around oval tracks. Having a larger right rear tire helps the car go faster. The V-8 engine produces up to 800 **horsepower** (HP). However, sprint cars are very light, and all that power can make them flip over. Wings help keep the cars on the track at high speeds.

Fast Fact

The wing on a sprint car is like an upside-down airplane wing. Instead of lifting the car up, it forces the car down. The end plates make turning the car easier.

Driver Joey Saldana leads a race at Volusia Speedway Park in Daytona Beach, Florida.

BULLRINGS

Sprint cars race on oval dirt tracks called bullrings. Some are a quarter mile (0.4 km) long, and some are a half mile (0.8 km) long. The dirt isn't like the dirt you find in a garden. Most tracks are made of clay mixed with a little water. This mix gets very sticky so that sprint car tires can grip the track better. Preparing a track for racing can take several hours. Water tankers, scrapers, and graders circle the track, making it just right for the race.

The first sprint car races were held at county fairs on the same dirt areas where livestock were displayed. That's why the tracks came to be called bullrings.

Fast Fact Knoxville Raceway—home to the Sprint Car Hall of Fame—is one of the oldest dirt tracks in America. Its first race was held in 1914.

SPRINT CARS ON THE TRACK

Racing a sprint car requires special practice and knowledge. Drivers must know how to slide sideways into corners and slingshot out of them onto the straight parts of the track to get into a winning position. Preparing the car for a race also takes experience. Teams must know what gears, wings, and tires will work best with each racetrack's dirt. Crew chiefs, mechanics, and drivers who master the art of preparing their cars win the most races.

During a race in 2010, driver Cody Darrah slides his sprint car around a turn.

13

RACE TIME!

During a sprint car event, drivers compete in time trials and short races to **qualify** for the main race. A driver who's fast enough wins a spot in the A-main, which is the final race. Some slower drivers win a spot in the B-main, which is a semifinal race. The top four drivers in the B-main make it into the A-main. An A-main has 25 to 40 laps to see who is the king of the bullring!

Fast Fact The "Kings Royal" is a famous yearly sprint car race held at the Eldora Speedway in Ohio. It's only a half-mile (0.8 km) track, but it can seat more than 20,000 fans.

Eldora Speedway

The A-main race is often the most exciting and the closest race of the night.

SPRINT CARS

BETWEEN RACES

Sprint car racing has a lot of bumping and banging, so the cars get pretty beat up. In addition, the dirt on a track changes a lot during a race. The sprint cars tear it up and dry it out. The **pits** at a sprint car race are very busy between races. Crews must repair the cars and adjust them to the changing conditions on the track. Getting the best **traction** on the dirt surface is the key to going faster.

Fast Fact Sprint car engines run on a fuel called **methanol**. It reduces the chance of explosions. A methanol fire can be put out with just water.

Driver Craig Dollansky (left) and a mechanic work on his car in the pits.

17

OUTLAW CHAMPS!

Steve "the King" Kinser holds the top records in the World of Outlaws (WoO) series. By the end of the 2009 racing season, he had 20 championships and 526 wins! He has also raced in the Indy 500 and in NASCAR races. Sammy Swindell has three WoO championships and the second-most WoO wins. Mark Kinser is a two-time WoO champion and holds the record for third-most all-time wins. Donny Schatz is fourth on the all-time wins list. He holds four WoO championships.

Many famous drivers in Indy Car and NASCAR got their start in sprint cars. These drivers include Mario Andretti, Tony Stewart, Jeff Gordon, and Sarah Fisher.

Steve Kinser poses with his award for winning the WoO 39th annual DIRTcar Nationals in 2010.

19

There's a lot of exciting bumping, sliding, and crashing in sprint car racing, but the cars are made to keep drivers safe. Strong safety cages, seats, and **safety harnesses** protect drivers and keep them in their cars in case of rollovers. Special safety helmets protect drivers' heads and necks. Parts like the wings and body panels are made to come apart during crashes to reduce the force on the drivers. So when you see parts flying off, that's good!

SPRINT CAR NUMBERS

Most WoO Wins	Steve Kinser, 561 (as of April 6, 2011)
Most WoO Championships	Steve Kinser, 20 (as of April 6, 2011)
First Woman to Win a WoO Race	Erin Crocker, Thunderbowl Raceway, October 2004
Fastest Average Lap Speed	David Steele, 144.167 miles (232.014 km) per hour, January 18, 1998

GLOSSARY

air pressure: the force of air pressing against something

assembly line: a system of manufacturing where workers and machines build a product part by part as it moves by them

horsepower: the measure of the power produced by an engine

mechanic: a person who builds and fixes cars

methanol: a liquid used as fuel in sprint cars

pits: a place near the track where cars get fuel and have problems fixed

qualify: to take part in events that will decide which drivers will be in the main race and what position they will start in

safety harness: several seat belts that work together to keep a driver safe in case of a crash

traction: the stickiness between two surfaces, such as a tire and the track

V-8 engine: a motor where two banks of four cylinders each are arranged in a V shape

wheelbase: the distance between the center of the front wheels and center of the back wheels

FOR MORE INFORMATION

Books

Schuette, Sarah L. *Sprint Cars.* Mankato, MN: Capstone Press, 2007.

Von Finn, Denny. *Sprint Cars.* Minneapolis, MN: Bellwether Media, 2009.

Websites

National Sprint Car Hall of Fame & Museum
www.sprintcarhof.com
Read about the legends of sprint car racing.

World of Outlaws Sprint Car Series
www.woosprint.com
Stay up to date on your favorite WoO drivers and teams.

INDEX